P Is for Pterodactyl*

*THE WORST ALPHABET BOOK EVER**

**All the letters that misbehave and make words nearly impossible to pronounce.

RAJ HALDAR & CHRIS CARPENTER   PICTURES BY MARIA TINA BEDDIA

sourcebooks
jabberwocky

Did you know that there are some really wacky words that start with a silent letter? Most of the time you can just ignore that pesky first letter and sound out the rest of the word. But be careful! There are other words in this book that don't follow the rules! Look to the back of the book for help with some of the most mischievous words.

Text copyright © 2018 by Raj Haldar and Chris Carpenter
Cover and internal illustrations © 2018 by Maria Tina Beddia
Cover and internal design © 2018 by Sourcebooks, Inc.

Sourcebooks and the colophon are registered trademarks of Sourcebooks, Inc.

The artwork was drawn by hand with ink and colored digitally.

Published by Sourcebooks Jabberwocky, an imprint of Sourcebooks, Inc.
P.O. Box 4410, Naperville, Illinois 60567–4410
(630) 961-3900
Fax: (630) 961-2168
sourcebooks.com

Library of Congress Cataloging-in-Publication data is on file with the publisher.

Source of Production: 1010 Printing International, North Point, Hong Kong, China
Date of Production: November 2019
Run Number: 5017022

Printed and bound in China.
OGP 15 14 13 12 11

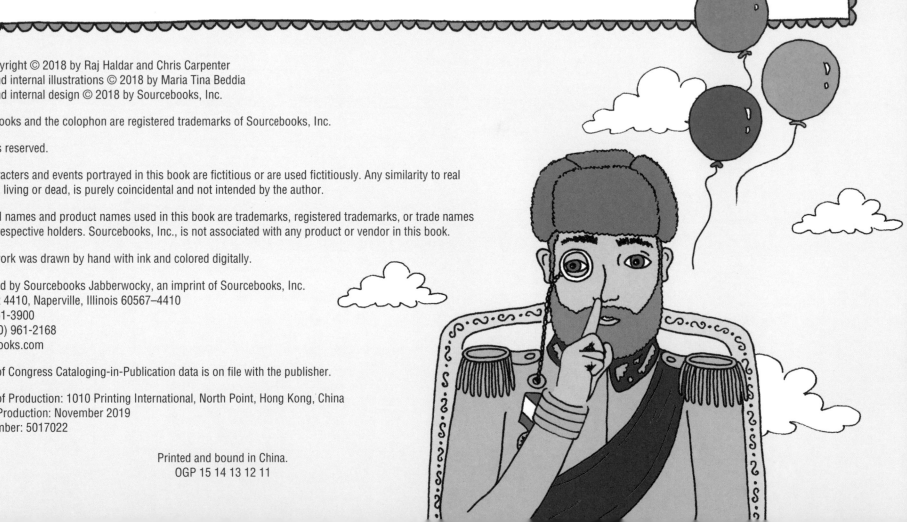

The bread aisle has not been cleaned in aeons,
and nine tiny beasts meet to have a feast.

We doubt anyone knows what bdellium is, but it's the only word dumb enough to begin with a silent B.

C is for Czar.

Shhh! The fascinating czar is secretly part Czech.

D is for Djibouti.

The boat race begins when the handsome judge from Djibouti drops his handkerchief from the bridge.

E is for Ewe.

Eileen the ewe was so euphoric the wolves
were eaten, she even gave the eulogy.

F is only for "foto" when you speak fluent Spanish at home!

G is for Gnocchi.

The gnome yells, "Waiter! There's a bright
white gnat nibbling on my gnocchi!"

H is for Heir.

The honest heir admits that herbalism isn't his cup of tea.

I is not for Eye.

We asked the pirate if he has two eyes, and he said, "aye, aye!"

J is for Jai Alai.

Juanita and Bjorn happily played jai alai
before eating fajitas in Juarez.

The noble knight's knife nicked the knave's knee.

An elephant named Elle rode the el train halfway to
El Paso and dined on hearts of palm with her folks.

But now Mr. M. can't remember why.

N is for naughty children who will sing a solemn
hymn when autumn comes to an end.

O is for Ouija.

The French leopard says, "Oui! We'd love to play
Ouija with the wee witch from Oaxaca."

P is for Pterodactyl.

Ptolemy the psychic pterodactyl struggles with psoriasis.

Q is for Quinoa.

We can enjoy quinoa and quiche by the quays of Qatar.

In England, the Queen proclaims, "We aren't saying the *r*'s in butterfly, shark, or lizard!"

S is for Seas.

Cee Cee swam through the debris in the seas to
see the imaginary isle of New Arkansas.

The charging tsunami washed away all of Tchaikovsky's tchotchkes.

U is not for You.

You never could have guessed that the wolf was disguised as the ewe!

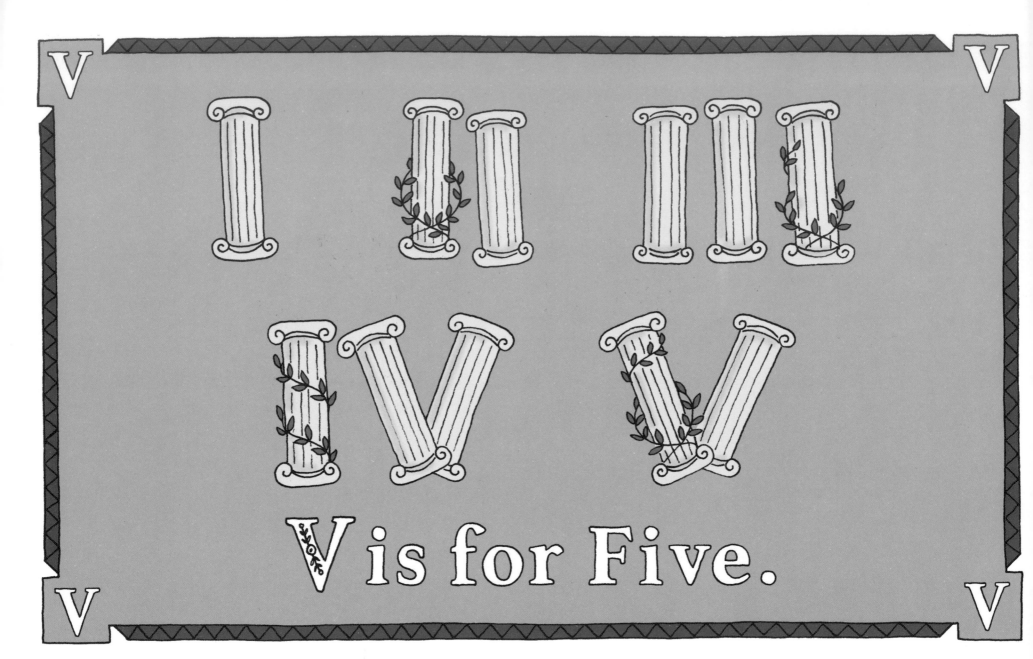

V is for Five.

How Roman-tic!

The wren wrapped the rabbit's gift in red, but forgot to write a note.

X is for Xylophone.

Xavier's extra arm made him an exceptional xylophone player.

But Yves, who is wearing yellow shorts, yells,
"Why is the Eiffel Tower upside down?"

Goodnight, Zhivago the zebra! I've enjoyed our rendezvous. Zzz...

And now... The Worst Glossary Ever!

Aisle (pronounced *I-yell*)—Any passage where people walk. Usually in grocery stores, airplanes, and movie theaters.

Autumn (pronounced *AWW-tum*)—The season after summer and before winter. It's also called "fall" because it's the time of year when leaves fall to the ground.

Aeon (pronounced *EE-yon*)—A very long period of time—say, back when the dinosaurs lived, or when you used to wear diapers!

Bdellium (pronounced *DEL-ee-yum*) is the good-smelling, sticky resin made by a specific species of tree that grows in parts of Africa and Asia. It is burned as incense in religious ceremonies around the world.

Czar (pronounced *zar*)—The title of a Russian ruler before 1917. Also can be used to describe any powerful person. After reading this book, you'll be the *czar of silent letters!*

Czech (pronounced *check*)—A person born or living in the Czech Republic, a country in Europe known for its castles.

Debris (pronounced *de-BREE*)—Broken pieces that are left after something has been destroyed.

The tiny African nation of **Djibouti** (pronounced *ja-BOO-tee*) is mostly desert, but the country is also home to Lake Assal—one of the saltiest bodies of water in the world!

El train (short for elevated train)—A railway with tracks above the street level. Commonly seen in big cities around the world.

El Paso (Spanish for *the Pass*)—A town in Texas that sits along the Rio Grande river at the U.S.-Mexico border.

Ewe (pronounced *you*)—A female sheep, like the ones lost by Little Bo Peep.

Euphoric (pronounced *you-FOUR-ick*)—Feeling very happy or excited, whether at your birthday party or after kicking the game-winning goal in a soccer game!

Eulogy (pronounced *YOU-luh-gee*)—A speech usually given at a funeral.

Exceptional (pronounced *eck-SEP-shun-ul*)—Much better than average; really good!

Foto (pronounced *PHO-toe*)—In Spanish, the "ph" in words like *ph*oto in English are spelled with an *f*. Tele*ph*one is teléfono, and even al*ph*abet is alfabeto! Isn't that phenomenal?

> What else comes from Spain? The city of Pamplona, Spain is famous for its Running of the Bulls, a tradition where feisty bulls chase brave runners through narrow streets.

Gnocchi (pronounced *NyO-key*)—Delicious little balls of dough that are boiled in water like dumplings and are usually served with a yummy sauce.

Gnome (pronounced *nome*)—A make-believe creature that looks like a little man and often wears a pointy hat.

Heir (pronounced *air*)—The person who is next in line to inherit something, such as a throne or fortune.

Herbalism (pronounced *ER-bal-is-um*)—The study of how plants can be turned into medicine.

Hymn (pronounced *him*)—A religious song that you might sing in a temple or church.

Isle (pronounced *I-yell*)—Shortened word for island. The country of Ireland is often called the Emerald Isle because it's so green!

Jai alai (pronounced *HIGH-lie*) is a sport that started in Spain and is played by using a scoop to throw a ball against a wall. It's called the "fastest sport in the world" because ball speeds can reach up to 188 miles per hour!

Knight (pronounced *night*)—A soldier from the Middle Ages who fought while riding a horse and wearing a full suit of armor.

> In modern times, knighthood or damehood is awarded to people who have accomplished something really special!

Knave (pronounced *nave*)—A dishonest person.

Knot (pronounced *not*)—What is formed when you tie a piece of string or rope to itself or to something else—just like those bunny ears on your shoelaces!

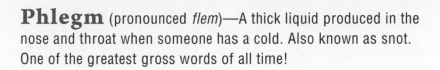

Mnemonic (pronounced *neh-MON-ic*)—A handy way of remembering something hard by connecting it to something easy. The next time you need to remember something, try making your own!

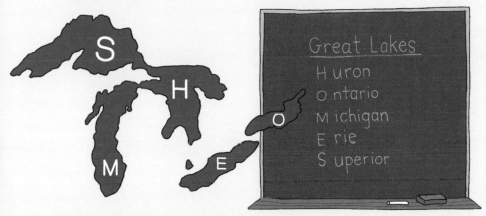

Oaxaca (pronounced *wa-HA-ka*) is a beautiful place in the southern part of Mexico.

Oui (pronounced *wee*)—The French word meaning "yes."

When a word starts with the silent letter *o* it usually makes a *w* sound. Oh, isn't the English language weird?

Ouija (pronounced *WEE-gee*) is a game that people play on Halloween.

Phlegm (pronounced *flem*)—A thick liquid produced in the nose and throat when someone has a cold. Also known as snot. One of the greatest gross words of all time!

Phooey (pronounced *FOO-wee*)—An exclamation used to express dislike for something.

Pterodactyl (pronounced *tair-o-DAC-tell*)—A huge flying dinosaur that lived a long time ago.

Who put the *p* in pterodactyl? The ancient Greeks! The word part "pter" is of Greek origin and means "winged" or "feathered," as in helico*pter*.

Ptolemy (pronounced *TOL-em-ee*)—A name that was popular in ancient times, most commonly associated with the Greek mathematician of the same name.

Psychic (pronounced *SIGH-kick*)—Used to describe someone with mysterious mental powers that can usually see the future.

Psoriasis (pronounced *so-RYE-ah-sis*)—A skin disease that causes areas of dry, itchy skin. Poor Ptolemy the pterodactyl!

Quinoa (pronounced *KEEN-wah*)—A round rice-like grain that's grown in South America.

Quiche (pronounced *keesh*)—A yummy pie made with eggs, milk, and cheese, often with veggies or meat added.

Quay (pronounced *key*)—The place where ships load and unload passengers on the land next to a body of water.

Qatar (pronounced *CUT-er*)—A country in the Middle East where there is lots of oil underground.

Rendezvous (pronounced *RON-day-voo*)—When people arrange a secret meeting at a particular time. Mysterious!

The British accent often skips over the *r* sound completely. If you want to speak like the Queen of England, just drop the *r*'s from words like *work, mark, for,* and *computer*, too!

Solemn (pronounced *SAH-lem*)—Very serious or formal in manner.

Of course the U.S. state of Arkansas is a real place! Its state bird is a mockingbird, and its official instrument is a fiddle. Arkansas is also home to the *only* diamond mine in the United States. Can you find these items on the *S* page?

Tsunami (pronounced *sue-NA-mee*)—A very large wave in the ocean that is usually caused by an earthquake. A tsunami can be even taller than a big building.

Tchaikovsky (pronounced *chai-COUGH-ski*)—The last name of Pyotr Ilyich Tchaikovsky, a famous classical musician from Russia.

Tchotchkes (pronounced *CHOCH-keys*)—A Yiddish word meaning an inexpensive souvenir or trinket.

Wren (pronounced *ren*)—A little bird that can be identified by its brown features and upward-pointing tail.

The Ancient Romans had an entirely different way of counting that used letters instead of numbers. It sounds hard, but it's easy as I, II, III. You may have noticed Roman numerals on old clocks and watches.

I	II	III	IV	V	VI	VII	VIII	IX	X
1	2	3	4	5	6	7	8	9	10

Xylophone (pronounced *ZY-la-phone*)—A musical instrument with wooden bars of different lengths that are struck with a mallet.

Zhivago (pronounced *jee-VAH-go*)—A Russian name that means "life," most commonly associated with the titular character from the book and movie, *Doctor Zhivago*.